I joyfully promise
to always be the best friend I can to all fairies.

I will use my voice to protect their natural world.
I will use my head to help them in their magic.
I will use my hands to care for them.
But most of all, I will use my heart to guard their secrets.

This I swear, by the power of happy ever afters.

MAGIC CAT PUBLISHING

The Secret Fairy Club © 2023 Lucky Cat Publishing Ltd
Text © 2023 Emma Roberts
Illustrations © 2023 Raahat Kaduji and Mira Miroslavova
First Published in 2023 by Magic Cat Publishing, an imprint of Lucky Cat Publishing Ltd
Unit 2 Empress Works, 24 Grove Passage, London E2 9FQ, UK
Magic Cat Publishing, an imprint of Lucky Cat Publishing Ltd,
PAKTA svetovanje d.o.o., Stegne 33, Ljubljana, Slovenia

The right of Emma Roberts to be identified as the author of this work and Raahat Kaduji and Mira Miroslavova to be identified as the illustrators of this work has been asserted by them in accordance with the Copyright, Designs and Patents Act, 1988 (UK).

No part of this publication may be reproduced, stored in a retrieval system, or transmitted, in any form, or by any means, electrical, mechanical, photocopying, recording or otherwise without the prior written permission of the publisher or a licence permitting restricted copying.

A catalogue record for this book is available from the British Library.

ISBN 978-1-915569-05-9

The illustrations were created using pen and ink, gouache and digital media
Set in Port Lligat, Duke Charming and Kingbirds

Published by Rachel Williams and Jenny Broom
Designed by Nicola Price and Sophie Gordon

Manufactured in China, TP1124

3 5 7 9 8 6 4 2

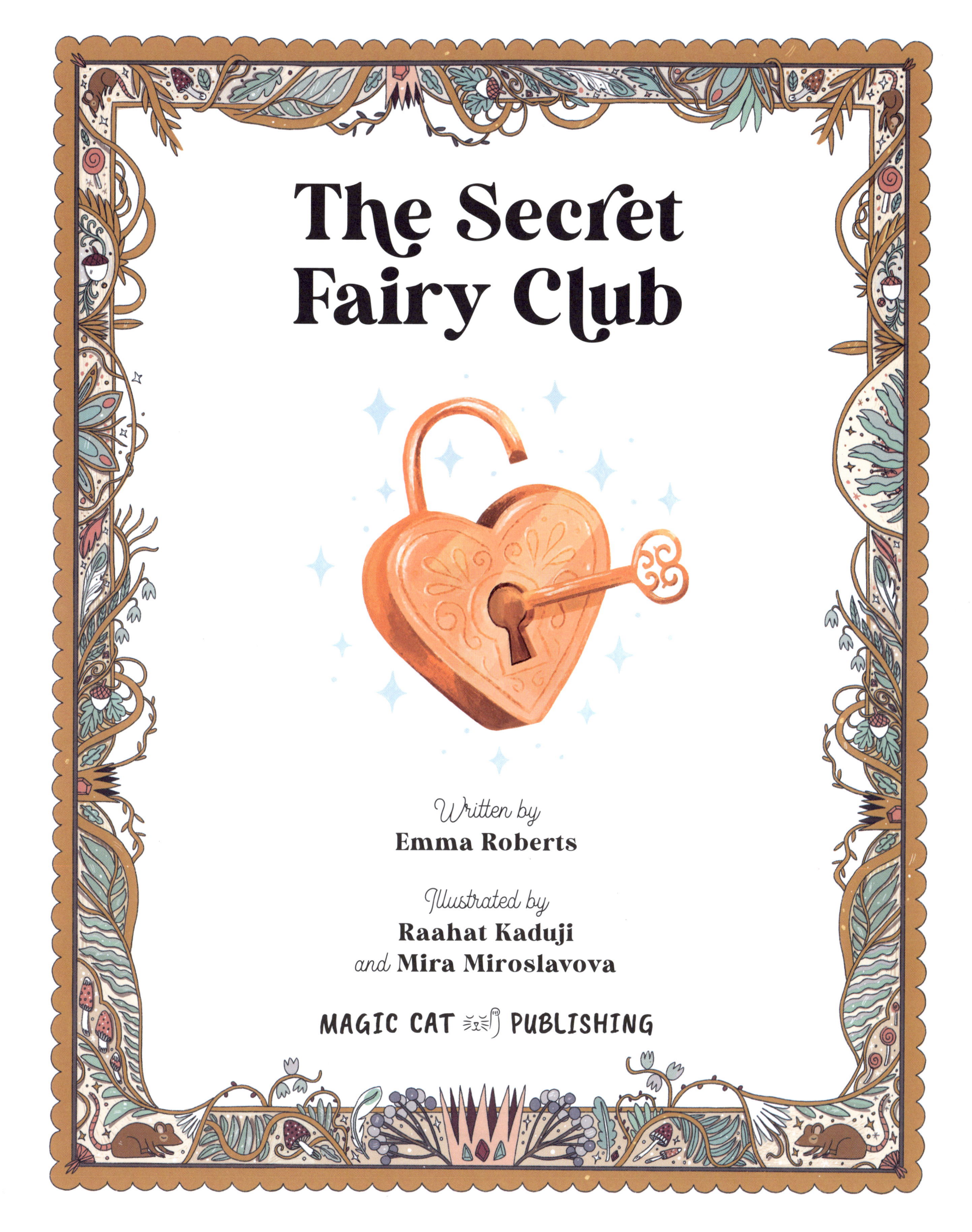

The Secret
Fairy Club

Written by
Emma Roberts

Illustrated by
Raahat Kaduji
and **Mira Miroslavova**

MAGIC CAT PUBLISHING

The Secret Fairy Club

Hello there, young human.

Do you believe in fairies?

You do... ? Very glad to hear it.

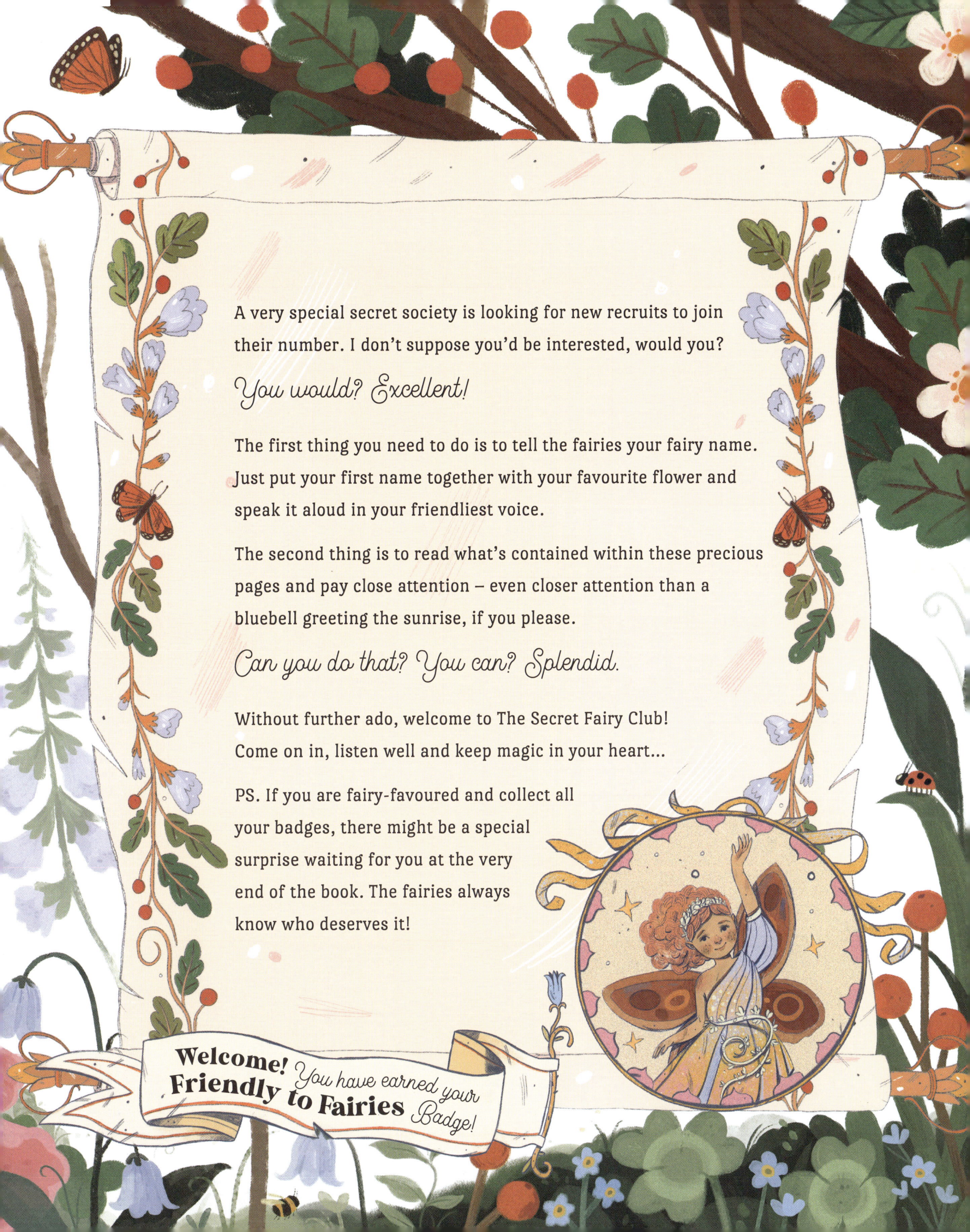

A very special secret society is looking for new recruits to join their number. I don't suppose you'd be interested, would you?

You would? Excellent!

The first thing you need to do is to tell the fairies your fairy name. Just put your first name together with your favourite flower and speak it aloud in your friendliest voice.

The second thing is to read what's contained within these precious pages and pay close attention – even closer attention than a bluebell greeting the sunrise, if you please.

Can you do that? You can? Splendid.

Without further ado, welcome to The Secret Fairy Club! Come on in, listen well and keep magic in your heart…

PS. If you are fairy-favoured and collect all your badges, there might be a special surprise waiting for you at the very end of the book. The fairies always know who deserves it!

Welcome! Friendly to Fairies *You have earned your Badge!*

Wings and Wonders

Meet the fairies

Greetings, friend of fairies, and welcome to a magical realm that is right on your doorstep... There are fairies everywhere in the human world and they can't wait to meet you.

Holding Shape
The wings of a fairy will always resemble those of their favourite flying creature.

Dragonfly wings
Fairies who have four dragonfly wings are champion flyers and can hover on the spot for hours at a time.

Hummingbird wings
Fairies with hummingbird wings can make music by beating their wings in particular patterns.

Ladybird wings
The protective shell of ladybird wings provides a handy shelter for fairies and their creature friends.

Lovely Locks

Every fairy's hair is unique and needs help from nature's treasures to keep it healthy. Here's what one fairy uses to look after their locks:

A spritz of warm dewdrops for plenty of moisture.

Precious oil from rare orchids for deep conditioning.

A porcupine-quill comb for styling.

A bonnet made from a silkworm's cocoon for sleeping in.

Butterfly wings
A fairy with butterfly wings can easily hide in nature, or give great joy with their colours and patterns.

Hooray! You have earned your Fairy **Goodness** Badge!

A baby fairy – a fairyling – is born every time something good happens in the world. Fairies' wings are their pride and joy, but fairylings only sprout theirs after they've granted their first wish.

Frills and Fripperies

Inside a fairy wardrobe

A fairy's fashion choices are inspired by the beauty of the natural world around them. Fairies adore making their own clothes and nature happily lends them bits and pieces to create looks from. What would you pick out to wear from the fairy wardrobe?

ACCESSORIES

gingko earrings

clover pendant

moonbeam necklace

Spanish bluebell bag

CLOTHES

myrtle-bark bolero

pansy party dress

Fabled and Fabulous

The Sugar Plum Fairy

There is one fairy whose fashion is unique among fairykind. She is famous for her edible outfits, though no one is ever allowed to take even a nibble! She's the Sugar Plum Fairy, and can be recognized by her gowns crafted from fondant icing or her trademark treacle-toffee hat and candy-cane umbrella. If you encounter the Sugar Plum Fairy, be sure to curtsey as deeply as you can and have some strawberry sherbet ready to offer her.

SHOES

- daisy bonnet
- buttercup bonnet
- conker cap
- unicorn top hat
- acorn hat
- stardust cap

HATS

Strike a pose. *You have earned your* **Fairy** *Fashion Badge!*

Town and Country

Fairies all around us

One of the best-kept secrets of the club is that we are never more than a few metres away from a fairy, wherever we live. Some fairies are happiest in the peace of the countryside and others thrive in the bustling city, with some moving between both, according to the seasons.

Hedgerow Fairies

Hedgerow fairies know how important hedges are to wildlife. These fairies keep busy in their hedgerows, helping creatures to find tasty treats and safe places for a snooze. But country fairies also love to help humans to enjoy the countryside too, making sure they don't get lost on the paths and trails!

In Town

Traffic-light fairies have bundles of energy and excellent eyesight. They work hard to help keep the busy roads safe. Gardener fairies make sure that all greenery in towns and cities will grow and flourish. Don't forget to whisper a thank-you to the city fairies when you're crossing at the lights or passing a balcony window box!

You clever thing! You have earned your Finding Fairies Badge!

Cloud Castles and Dainty Dwellings

At home with fairies

Fairies will make their homes in places that give them joy and make their wings flutter. It is vital to keep the location of fairy communities top secret, as fairies don't want nosy humans poking around! Members of The Secret Fairy Club will always be welcome, however.

bed-chamber

library

throne room

bathing room

carriage house

cold store

The Three Fairy Godmothers of the Northern Skies have graciously allowed you a peek inside their sparkling palace, hidden in the clouds.

Deep within the oldest, gnarliest tree of the forest, you'll find a Woodland Fairy's happy place.

passage

loft store

potting shed

kitchen

To be able to cross a fairy threshold, a human must first:
- do a star jump with nicely pointed toes;
- hum a cheery tune;
- burp the alphabet, backwards.

Pull up a chair! *You have earned your* **Fairy Home and Hearth** *Badge!*

pantry

Hazelnuts and Hibernation

Nature's tiny helpers

Helping the hazel dormouse

Spring
When a sleepy dormouse emerges from hibernation, a fairy will always be there, waiting, with a gift of food. Wild cherries and hawthorn blossom are big favourites for the first meal of spring.

Winter
These fairies are expert builders, helping the dormice to gather materials to create their warm and cosy nest on the forest floor. The fairies tuck the dormice in and kiss them goodnight for the winter.

Because of climate change leading to warmer winters, dormice sometimes wake up earlier than they should, before there's food available. The forest fairies do everything they can to help, but we, as The Secret Fairy Club, must pledge to care for our planet to help the dormice and all other creatures who are under threat.

Fairies will do anything to help the wildlife living around them, and for some, it's a job that lasts all year round. Come and take a peek into the lives of the Forest Fairies who care for the animals who are their friends and neighbours.

Summer

With the arrival of summer comes the birth of baby dormice. A Forest Fairy will stop by for a cuddle with the adorable babies and to check the new dormouse parents have everything they need.

Autumn

It's time to feast and put on lots of body fat to last a dormouse through the long winter snooze. Fairies deliver takeaways to their dormouse friends, including scrummy nuts and berries.

Aren't you great? You have earned your **Wildlife Helpers** Badge!

Healing Spells and Wish-You-Wells

The fairy wildlife hospital

Where can the local wildlife go when they're sick? The fairy hospital, of course! Here, the fairies will nurse their animal friends back to health with the help of healing spells and natural remedies. As a Secret Fairy Club member, you can add strength to the spells by saying them out loud.

Blue tit
Broken wing: ice-skating on a frozen puddle

Frog
Tummy ache: eating too many flies

Whoops-a-daisy, you fell down
and now you're feeling sore.
With fairy help and healing words,
let's make your pain no more!

When chomping snacks it's hard to stop,
especially when they're yummy.
I speak this precious magic spell
to soothe your poorly tummy.

You're a hero! You have earned your Fairy **Healing** Badge!

Ladybird

Bumped head: Flying into a window

Squirrel

Trapped tail: rolling down hills (for fun!)

Did you fly a bit too fast?
You've taken quite a bump.
Trust in fairy medicine;
we'll help you with that lump.

Stuff's got stuck in places
where it really shouldn't be.
We'll cast this spell of liberty
and set your tail free!

Starry Nights and Party Delights

How to get ready for a fairy ball

What luck – you've been invited to the most special night of the year, Queen Titania's annual ball! Every member of The Secret Fairy Club must lend a hand to prepare. Maybe you can find some useful party-planning tips in *Spangles!*, the fairies' favourite magazine?

Want to dance all night but worried about aching wings? Try all-new Flippety-Flap Soothing Balm! Just one drop on each wing tip and you'll be the last to leave the ballroom...

Feasts Fit for a Queen!

Want to make Titania's taste buds tingle? Try these tantalizing recipes and be star baker at the ball.

Mooncakes

(Makes: 75)

1 ball of chestnut butter
2 drops of daydreams
A pinch of popping candy

Combine all ingredients by the light of the full moon. Bake in a volcano and leave to cool for 20 minutes before eating.

Elven Bread

(Makes: as many loaves as you need)

2 treasure chests of tree bark
1 barrel of cloud milk
3 griffin eggs

Stir briskly, then leave dough to rise for a month in a happy place. For best results, cook over live dragon fire.

Light Up the Room

Humans call their party lighting 'fairy lights'. Try our top three ideas for actual fairy lights:

- Glow-worms
- Lanternfish 
- Fireflies 

Always ask the creature's permission first!

Your Wardrobe Made Fabulous

All fairies get a front-row seat for the fashion show of the year! Here's how to magic your old wardrobe into new party-wear...

Shoes
Crystals are last year's sparkle. Pick them off and save in a jar for next season. It's all about spider-silk bows this year...

Jewellery
Want to give your precious trinkets new life for the ball? Paint them in rainbow dust and they'll be sure to catch the queen's eye!

Bags
Try swapping your bag with one belonging to a fairy friend. They'll get something 'new' and so will you!

First time at the ball? Let *Spangles!* magazine's very own fairy godmother give you her wise advice.

Q: Should I bring a gift for Queen Titania?

A: Your presence at the ball is present enough for our queen. But I happen to know that she is partial to a jar of honeysuckle marmalade, should you wish to win her favour...

Q: Can I bring a pet?

A: Will your pet set fire to anything — accidentally or otherwise? If so, leave them safe and snug at home. None of us want singed wings.

Q: How much is a ticket?

A: The fairy ball is always free to attend. It's Queen Titania's kind gift to us all. However, there will be a charity collection for the Retired Robins Trust, and all spare acorns will be gratefully received.

Your spangles are sparkling! You've earned your *Party* Badge!

Shimmy and Shine

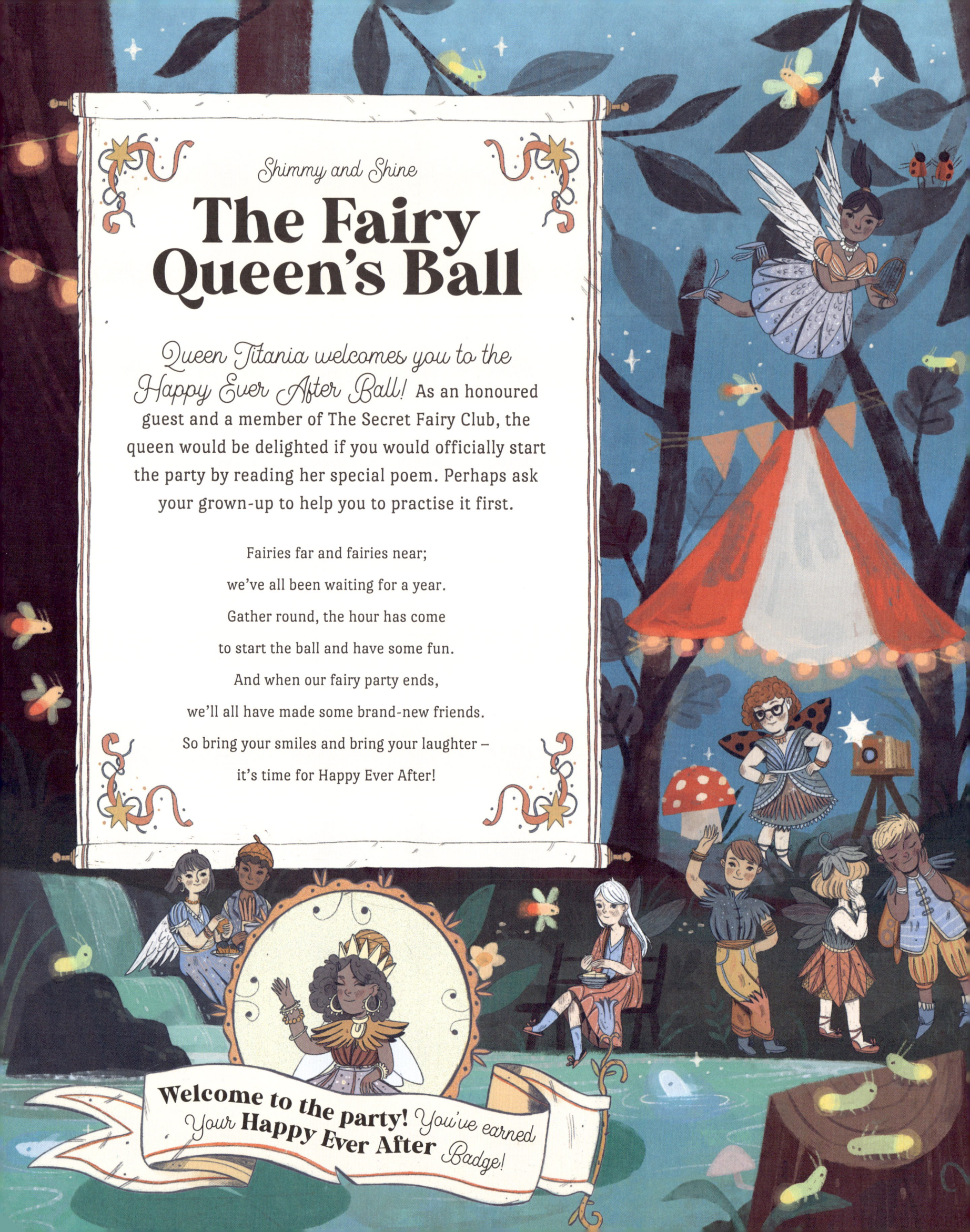

The Fairy Queen's Ball

Queen Titania welcomes you to the Happy Ever After Ball! As an honoured guest and a member of The Secret Fairy Club, the queen would be delighted if you would officially start the party by reading her special poem. Perhaps ask your grown-up to help you to practise it first.

Fairies far and fairies near;
we've all been waiting for a year.
Gather round, the hour has come
to start the ball and have some fun.
And when our fairy party ends,
we'll all have made some brand-new friends.
So bring your smiles and bring your laughter –
it's time for Happy Ever After!

Welcome to the party! *You've earned* Your **Happy Ever After** *Badge!*

THE HAPPY EVER AFTER BALL

Fantabulous!

You have collected all your badges and are almost the newest member of The Secret Fairy Club...

Now you must take the ancient oath of the club, and then a very special secret will be revealed. So, blow a kiss to the fairies who live around you, flap your arms like wings and say these words with magic in your heart:

I, ..., joyfully promise to always be the best friend I can to all fairies.

I will use my voice to protect their natural world.
I will use my head to help them in their magic.
I will use my hands to care for them.
But, most of all, I will use my heart
to guard their secrets.

This I swear, by the power of happy ever afters.

Are you ready for a very special secret, shared only with club members? Go to the back to discover the treasure hidden within...

Official Secret Fairy Club Member

Here is your tenth badge, which unlocks your membership to **The Secret Fairy Club!**